Catullan Games

Sándor Rákos

Catullan Games

Translated from Hungarian
by Jascha Kessler and Maria Körösy

The Marlboro Press

Originally published in Hungarian as
CATULLUSI JÁTÉKOK
Copyright © 1984 Szépirodalmi

The publication of the present volume is made possible by a
grant from the National Endowment for the Arts.

Manufactured in the United States of America

Library of Congress Catalog Card Number 89-60942

ISBN 0-910395-53-5

The Marlboro Press
Box 157
Marlboro, VT 05344

Acknowledgments

Excerpts from *Catullan Games* have appeared in *Translation* (New York), *PEN International* (London), and *Arion 15* (Budapest).

The translator wishes to thank not only his collaborator of many years, Maria Körösy, for all the effort and time she has always so generously offered, but also the Hungarian P.E.N. Club, and its former Secretary General, Professor László Kéry, who may truly be called *the onlie begetter* of this work. Through seven courteous invitations to Budapest ever since 1972, their support and attention have made it possible to become personally acquainted with so many excellent poets as well as affording the privilege of attempting to carry over as much of their poetry as I could into American.

Contents

Catullus and Catullan Games

When in the middle of the first century B.C. Catullus addressed himself with the epithet *miser Catulle*, he had available to him a well-grounded, epic-tragic tradition of serious verse that had been developed for over two hundred years, as well as a less coherent tradition of comic-satiric poetry. The latter derived from a fusion of the elements of comic drama with colloquial language, and was characterized by the somewhat personal tone exhibited in Roman republican satire, which was to be powerfully exploited by Juvenal and Martial later on. Also fashionable during the last period of the Republic was the epigram, a genre modelled on the practice of well-known classical and Alexandrian writers who wrote for the amusement of sophisticated patrons. These were quite short poems on subjects such as love and lovers, prominent personalities, and what might be called criticism, a blend of backbiting gossip and literary chatter that revolved about the praise/damnation of plays and books. As Kenneth Quinn tells us in *The Catullan Revolution*, all three forms of verse were blended and reshaped by the poet into something new. The *Carmina* are unprecedented in Latin literature.

Born in Verona to a family of good standing (his father was someone able to entertain Caesar), Catullus lived from about 84 to 54 B.C. As Quinn understands it, he seized the opportunity afforded by the newly-wealthy Roman society of his day to speak informally of himself and for himself, rather than sing to the community as its bard and/or instructor. The New Poets of the middle decades of the first century abjured the grander convention of Latin tradition that informed the expectation of their elders, choosing to write for a circle of friends, even for their own amusement. They wanted to make a new kind of poem and make it well: they aimed at precision and economy of statement, packing their texts with learning carried as lightly and flourished as easily as a walking stick. Brilliant expression was what those poets strove for. Personal and immediate, theirs is fresh, unofficial conversation offered by individuals to individuals. Such poetry, spoken almost as an aside to cognoscenti, is a compound of irony, wit, mockery. When they criticized power their satire was intensely personal, and not wielded as the weapon of a patrician class resentful of the rise of powerful men like Pompey or Caesar. The poetry of Catullus and his peers, a privileged group, was an intense, self-conscious, youthful and high-spirited thing; it was coterie verse, vers de société, and it certainly turned away from the high serious, which, descending from Ennius and practiced at that time by, say Cicero, twenty to twenty-five years their senior, stood for the traditional understanding of the epical in Latin poetry. Yet there is also in Catullus a refinement of technique and language that set a new, high standard for the work of the Augustans of the next generation. In short, the genius of Catullus, as Quinn concludes, was original.

The intense interest in the *Carmina* during the last forty years may be understood as a reminder that the unmeditated utterance of passion should not be taken as the sole premise of the lyrical in poetry. In fact, the representation of emotion is something Catullus invented for Latin. The artifice of his poetry comes not only from his own experience—but also his knowledge of the Greek poets whose work he absorbed, translated, and imitated, poets like Sappho and Archilochus, Callimachus and Theocritus. They can be read as the antique precursors to his matter, whereas it was the Hellenistic writers who informed his manner. Their recombination produces, so far as is known, something found in Latin first and fully in Catullus.

What we take to be the elemental emotions sound clearly in his verses, whether it be the laughter of delight in the joy of the moment, together with its complements, the poignancy of recollection and lamentation over its passing, or the mutter of contempt and hatred, with their complements, the sneer of scorn and the cacchination of the curse. On reflection, however, we realize that they are but replications of emotion, not the ingenuous outcry of passion. Instead of the direct expression of the very person at the instant of feeling, the primordial voicing that is the *song* of the song, as it were. What we have in Catullus is passion sublimated, objectified, rendered formally as elegy and epigram, narrative and miniature "epic," learnèd nuptial song and diatribe, and not the delicate, "natural" lyric of Sappho. It is an artful poetry, a poetry self-consciously practiced, and so sophisticated it both reveals its agonist and conceals that *other* person who composes poems, someone who may be the *true* self. . . or may not. What-

[xii]

ever the case, the Catullus who helplessly suffers the disasters of love is not hapless: there is also the poet who observes his own rage, desire, misery, disgust, just as he observes friend and enemy and all those comings and goings marked by the absurd yet charming contingency of any ordinary day to which a man called Catullus wakes—and the night into which he walks. In short, the Catullan self-revelation is that of a persona. It may be said therefore that the poet mediates between two connoisseurs of catastrophe: the one who hates and loves, and the one who knows he hates and loves. Perhaps the poet too is another, one of "so many Catulluses," as "Epilogue I" of the *Catullan Games* puts it: simply a mask worn by the soul, that unknown, unknowable intelligence, which is the ultimate ground of our being in this world.

The Latin's poetic works have been translated often and variously into English, and the contemporary scholiast and critic have said novel things concerning them. Certainly much of what we have been told illuminates our appreciation of modern poetry, because we can imagine both the persona and the presumed person of Catullus as somehow contemporary, even if all other things that discriminate periods separated by two thousand years are scarcely equal. A poet who is able at once to study his own psychology and write of it by seeming to write out of it will always be extraordinary. Yet more admirable, when he can speak of himself *as* himself, shamelessly if you will, but with a modest, ingenuous candor more convincing than his tough-minded, even cynical follower Ovid attained. As for some of our twentieth century poets writing in English— a Yeats, a Graves, a Pound, an Eliot, a Stevens, or even that insouciant Cummings—they could never have hoped to attempt it. Neither does Baudelaire, or Trakl, or Benn exhibit such qualities, though they were each in their own way morbidly obsessed. As for the anguish of Rilke, by the light of Catullus it appears to have been sublimated into nostalgia for the metaphysical sublime. As for our recent American "confessional poetry," its signature is stereotypically pathological, in other words marked by a fundamentally dissociated suffering. One thinks of Lowell, Berryman, and Plath, for example, whose anguish wears the mask of madness. It was not Eros or Aphrodite that plagued them: the collective Muse these poets courted and paid obeisance to were those punishers the Erïnyes, Patronesses of Paranoia.

[xiii]

Most attractive to us in Catullus is the poet who bravely claims his right to autonomy in a dangerous, unstable time, who stands on the shifting ground between the virtues of a venerable past and the emerging complexity of an imperial society in which, as Hamlet later observed of his uncle's, Claudius' court at Elsinore, death can strike one from a little hole drilled in the wall. Such a voice we recognize and respect, for we realize we cannot hope to hold ourselves as self-possessed as it seems Catullus could and did. Even though we have known the terror of utter vulnerability in our time and have experienced the obliteration of the human, we have not quite understood how it might be possible to speak of it. Therein lies the essential difference between our time and that of the young Veronese. The Judeo-Christian civilization long ago absorbed the Classical world, transforming absolutely and forever the notion of what the person was in 60 B.C. We live moreover at its end, when its history is for us only . . . history. After such knowledge, it can only be said that when we peruse the *Carmina* today we realize that the lucid person we call Catullus, whose persona we so exteem in the immediacy of his (auto) biography, is simply irrecoverable. We sense that most poignantly. And yet—

—Yet here is Sándor Rákos. What are we to make of his *Catullan Games*? Rather than attempting a versified resumé of the scholarship interpreting the social context and commenting on the vicissitudes of the years 64-54 B.C. that appear to underlie the subtle Latin text, the Hungarian poet has dared to assume a voice for the persona of Catullus as one might imagine it can be heard in the *Carmina*. At first glance such a project would appear supererogatory. We wouldn't be surprised were some novelist to concoct a scabrous narrative pretending to evoke Rome during the "twilight of the Republic." That sort of junket into the remote past is all-too fashionable today. In the hands of a Henry Treece or Robert Graves, both fine poets, the historical novel can offer the simulacrum of a living voice, even though those writers usually ventriloquize for heroes either real or mythological, heroes who had no voice. But to write a novel about a poet as exquisitely articulate as Catullus would result I think in that familiar, flabby and merely sensational best-seller prose which is the merely pornographic product of industrious "research." Anything's possible, of course, and such a project is probably in the works somewhere right now even though it could prove hard to find the publisher to take an interest in a *poet*, especially such an unsentimental poet as Catullus, who wrote poems "as cold and clear as the dawn." A sophisticated publisher, himself a quondam poet, perused this translation of Rákos and was angry with me that *Catullan Games* had been written! He told me it sufficed him to know the Latin poems. I was astonished by his attitude, which struck me as both snobbish and obtuse. It had led him, comically enough, into (mis)reading Rákos's *Catullan Games* as a pseudo-translation of the *Carmina*! which is obviously neither the Hungarian's intention nor his unintended achievement.

Or, perhaps the question is not that obvious. Why does Sándor Rákos fabricate an approximation of the mask worn in the *Carmina*? Why imitate or counterfiet a persona for the poet who told Rome how he hated and loved someone called Lesbia, whose original is thought to have been one Clodia, a rich and powerful married woman ten years older than he was. That Catullus, who appears to have died at around thirty years of age, remains immutably concealed behind the portrait he left of himself. What is Rákos *saying* by assuming such a mask? What purpose may it serve? The answer is, *Catullan Games* does not propose itself as a surrogate for the original.

I think the reader of these poems will find that the Hungarian artist has fairly limited himself to the poet's "main business," the twin themes of hate and love. His little book introduces us in "Prologue I" to the "Grand Games of the Groin," opening immediately upon the torments of Eros and the fascination by Lesbia. His intense meditations on love's war and his fantasies of a possible other course of life are followed in the latter third of the sequence by poems in which Rákos offers a passing, penetrant glance at the society that was the background for the *Carmina*, exhibiting the poet as literary satirist and politically-conscious, even self-destructive victim of an increasingly cynical and corrupt society. The Catullus of the *Games* puts the threat of execution for outspokenness in the mouth of still another poet who, or so he pretends, has sent him an admonitory letter begging him to omit his friends' names from his jibes because the tyrant will have their heads too. Earlier we have read a letter from Lesbia accusing her lover of selfish egotism, a letter that Rákos suggests he probably wrote and addressed to himself. False (auto)biography is what we have here. But after

[xv]

all, our Catullus is now writing in twentieth century Hungarian. (Yet the note to Lesbia's letter consists of quotations from a translation of genuine Catullus into Hungarian by Gábor Devecseri, the classicist who was a friend of Robert Graves!) On the other hand, there are also clues planted suggesting the fiction that Catullus, not Sándor Rákos, was really the writer of the poems in *Catullan Games*; for example the notes by some scribal editor (Sándor Rákos who else?) informing the reader that parts of the original MS. have been torn away at moments of violent emotion. But whose? The MSS. from the 1300's that came down as the writings of Catullus? In other words, are those texts copied by scribal annotators? Are they Rákos's texts? In short, in speaking Catullus, and speaking of Catullus in Hungarian, Rákos has done what only a modern is able to do: he has identified psychologically with that virtual Catullus—the Catullus who seems to exist in the *Carmina*—, has entered him in order to *re*-present him, going so far as to have his (fictive) young Italian from Verona produce the various personae who satirize him in the *Games*. These are Masks worn over masks: it is a kind of psychoanalysis, all the more unusual in that it is a *self*-analysis conducted in verse dramatically, his affairs are given as current event and not memories recollected in tranquility.

Even so vivid a self-portrait by the persona Philip Roth produced for us in *Portnoy's Complaint*, for example, is offered retrospectively. Portnoy pores over his childhood and adolescence, trying to explain himself: he may know what he was, but Roth's reader knows it will take him forever to discover what he is. Catullus, however, seems to have known just that: the *Carmina* are proof; whereas in Portnoy's end is only his beginning. The reader will recall that elaboration of Portnoy's true character is to commence *after* the last sentence of the novel; in other words, it remains unwritten. Moreover, that (potential) conversation must be imagined as a confessional game—that of the psychoanalysis with one Dr. Spielvogel. Incidentally, "Spiel" means game, and "Vogel" a bird; used, as a verb, "Vögel'n" is a well-worn slang expression for the games of sex: "Vögel'n" means to hunt after, to do the act itself, in American slang "to screw around," and "screw." Portnoy's doctor is named not only onomastically, but the choice of his name is over-determined: the analyst is in fact the mirror of and for the analysand, and it can be said that psychoanalysis is the art of confession, as for that matter is writing itself. The agon endured in art may be a game; yet game or not, when it is played honestly it proves interminable—just as does your true psychoanalysis. And that incidentally suggests why there are *three* Epilogues closing the *Catullan Games:* the analysis of poem and poet will continue after the end, going on indeed into eternity.

Of course, such a mode of self-dramatization, of self-excoriation as Rákos offers does imitate the achievement of Catullus—except for the explicitly analytical cast the twentieth century will ineluctably contribute to autobiography. It may be retorted that the Catullus of the *Carmina* is similarly selfconscious. So he is. But in that case the poet who knows he plays games, as does the speaker of Rákos' poem, may be said to be super-selfconscious, inasmuch as he is present as a modern writer commenting on the *Carmina,* dividing them into sets of games, arranged in categories that define and disclose our distancing from our own emotions, left as we are to endure passions in the condition of anxious detachment from ourselves, in an agon dissolved by the acid of knowingness . . . as Nietzsche might have put it. It makes for bitter comedy, both a little more and a little less than the proper and lovely self-possession of our original, the Catullus of the *Carmina.*

In other words, the *Carmina* are by no means what is offered here. Rákos is saying that they are to be read through the long perspective of centuries, that perhaps we can only read towards the *Carmina* through the *Catullan Games*! A startling prospect! Furthermore, Rákos exhibits Catullus' art through a discontinuous perspective; it is as though the time between his disappearance and the recovery of the manuscript in Verona were to be folded like a sheet of parchment so that the edge that marks the closure of the *Carmina* with silence is broken after a thousand years when it is joined to the pious gloss written "against that barbèd-voiced" Ancient by a naive cleric, and we encounter the poet again after the hiatus of many centuries. Certainly he is viewed oddly and askance by this medieval scribe whose response is a crude if charming homily in favor of Woman. Such a Christian view of the Latin's passion serves to illuminate the chasm between the ancient world and ours: the scribe, whose quatrains cannot overleap the distance between the classical ethos and his, scarcely even realizes that the reciting of Paternosters from now till Doomsday can never save nor even salve the soul of that poor Catullus he deems resident in Hell (whose gates opened once for Christ—and once for Alighieri—and will never open again). Rákos' comedy is subtle. And there is more: the mask of that medieval scribe overlies or covers contrapuntally the facsimile of an eighteenth century Hungarian poet named Csokonai—another learned love-obsessed, love-doomed poet . . . *miser Csokonai*! one can almost hear Catullus groan.

Which brings us to the present, and our awareness that there is also a poet named Sándor Rákos, who in a final group of poems proposes a last word on Catullus. As though to offer yet more masks, one poem, "The Resurrection of the Poet Catullus," is marked as an MS. discovery taken from the back of a page supposed to have been inscribed with an unknown set of verses on "The Death of the Poet Catullus"! The implication, of course, is that the Veronese never died; or if he did, the scholiast, our commentator-poet, is adding a hymn of praise meant to say, Though Catullus be dead, long live Catullus! Following that poem, we find the savage quatrains of "Dissecting Kisses," set out as a pair of simultaneous poems in which a raging ghost mutters to Lesbia, addressed directly as "you" as if she were here reading these words with us. Here Rákos expresses the ultimate agony of the lover in whose thought is exposed the source of all love's distress: that we are and always have been obsessed, not by lust and the flesh, but with a longing to unite with the soul of our beloved, a soul enigmatic, secret, never to be known, even though it is a thing but conjured by art into (virtually) objective being—such being as words spoken by a voice in a poem may obtain.

Finally we reach "Epilogue III," in which we find Rákos speaking directly to his Catullus. He tells him how we think of him, expressing once and for all the ultimate ground of our relationship: "so you seal up/the solitary life of the dead and the living." When all is said and done, after the games, after the ashes of life itself have blown away on the wind of time, the shadow of Catullus hovers immanent over all of us who hate and love, always potentially incarnate in the inexpressible longing of our desire. After which, nothing remains but to hail the poet in our name: *frater ave atque vale*. The rest is silence.

—JASCHA KESSLER

Santa Monica
February 1989

[xviii]

Catullan Games

Prologue I

comrades-in-love
all you men and all you women
now enmeshed in Grand Games of the Groin
your sighs your groans your spasms
your swift recurrent fevers
might as well be ours and you too
could feel the current of our coupling
over hot wires laid between us
through no-man's-land
transmitting no voice that's human
just high-voltage sparking and beneath our beds
who knows what mine is about to go off
in this Age of Flaming Ice

Prologue II

poor Catullus a poet, by the way
his main business being the bitter investigation
of some devastating pandemic disease
known from time out of mind yet occasionally
taking variant forms
you said honey   you said wormwood   you said balm
you say fever   you say surfeit   you say religion
deathwish hopes of rising from the dead
a constructive and destructive power
always an enemy to common sense
everyone knows it   almost everyone's
somehow survived it
and still nothing is known about it
except that it recurs in us all
as if for the first time
no matter how often no immunity
we can carry the infection for a lifetime
and though it comes with feelings of exhilaration
and a deceptive sense of *singularity*
looking at it objectively it's always and everywhere
exasperatingly dull and the same
excluding mine and yours
and all those present for that matter
because you and I and they the three of them
that is both of us and humanity in general
are extraordinary exceptions in love and perhaps won't die
because this love of ours knows not death and our life
is the one-and-only never-before
the one-and-only never-again
unmatchable and unique
as is our grief and our misfortune too
so be it   *miser Catulle*

[3]

Love Games

a false alarm wakes me with a jerk
where am I where did I drop off
in the midst of that mad
uproar so I couldn't tell
if it was some temple or banquet in a brothel
that was making all the racket
someone approaches gesticulating
and reciting an incomprehensible soliloquy
someone else takes me by the arm and leads me aside
somewhere in a corner
a third comes with meat and wine
a fourth hawks a gob in my face
there's a hooknosed old man too with
a warning in his eagle eyes
and when I take a flop a whitehaired
matron stoops over me and   respectfully
I kiss her hand
how this woman beside me got here
and stuck to me so long I don't know anymore
she's suddenly here as though she's always been here
as though there's nowhere else for her to be
but at my side forever at my side
I gaze into her eyes she gazes into mine
                                        LESBIA
a light comes up lightning-clear for *one* moment
the chaos grows even darker then

I love you   you do hear me? *I* love you
I more you than you are   I   am *you*
unique among all the living
born for you alone the half that's whole together
we two   THE FULL EMBRACE

without you I'm maimed   you're maimed without me
a left missing its right   a right missing its left
me you could not   you I could not
ourselves we could not   EMBRACE
a stick has two ends
no matter how many times you halve it
so we are one another's end
bruising and breaking in two
and still two-in-one   though broken
striking ourselves struck by ourselves
the way a stick never hits itself
and blossoming too   blossoming
the way a stick never blossoms

when we two make love Lesbia
we stand on the two shores Lesbia
of the sea Lesbia
and when we are joined Lesbia
                    the sea roars
when we don't make love Lesbia
we stand on two cliffs Lesbia
below us an abyss Lesbia
between us no bridge Lesbia
              the cold wind blows

since this terrible disease
this insatiable pain has wasted me
as lonely in an ocean of people
as though in the sea's depths
yet if I sank to the floor of the sea
I'd be alone no more

just a gleam just half a
nod just a secret
wink of your eye
I can't ask it of your hand   it's another's

[6]

nor your mouth   it said yes to another
I can't ask them for a sign
but admit that even a dog
even a dog Lesbia merits a wink a pat
when its owner forgives   me only you
treat worse than your dog
you're silent though hate and love
torment me with your silence
oh god oh dear god you mighty
goddess of love how long must I bear
this agony   please give me a sign
you still love me Lesbia   some sign no matter
how slight   even a flutter of an eyelash

you don't believe that Catullus is prepared
to die for you Lesbia at a moment's notice
to have his throat slashed
his heart ripped out
you doubt it Lesbia of course you think it's too high a price
good gold he's paid out for copper
thrown his whole life away
for your phony feelings
but you can't comprehend it's not *for you*
not merely for you for your presumably
nowhere and non pareil
fire-purple love
your incendiary eyes
but for something else something more
that might be and is not
for a love whose fire's far grander
than your incendiary eyes
your fire-purple love
for therein lie all causes and all ends
for all ends and for all causes

[7]

Trust and Treachery Games

never was there a faithfulness so twinned
we're faithful as our own hands
born for   one another halves   a whole together
never such a one and only two-in-one
lacking you I'm maimed   you're maimed lacking me
a left that's lost its right   a right that's lost its left
me you could not   you I could not
ourselves we could not   EMBRACE
never was there a faithfulness so unique and so numberless
      more   than myself alone
      more   than yourself alone
      more than just we two
take care   *everything's* lost   if we should let go

                    I believed in you
                    like a child in its mother
                    the priest his god
                    the soldier the commander
                    a fleeing convict his cloak of night
                    an acrobat the high wire
                    dogs their masters
                    flocks their shepherd
                    barbarians their idol
                    peoples in their rights
                    only more so
                    YOU MOCKED MY FAITH
                    DAMN YOU

where are you when you're not when you're not
with me this immense city's
jungle pimps you how am I to know which
one of its streets has carried you off which threshold

has sucked you in what stairway and what
steps accompany you toward which
chamber and who awaits
you there and what is expected
of you only a job or something more besides
and if so
are you used
like a tool of your trade symbolically
or in the flesh as well does some other male's
face and do his parts illuminate you
and does the whip of four-letter words
lash your naked body from
head to toe

I'd hide myself   there is no place
they hound me everywhere
accost me in the vacant streets
grinning to my face
I blow out the taper at night
lie back in my hot bed
and all of them surround me those who were are and will be
my thousand jeering rivals

a rival's no worse
than I'd be if I sat where he's sitting
with you I'd do it too
that's why jealousy's such torture
I'm jealous of you   *because of myself*
you're jealous of me   *because of yourself*
we're jealous of love   *because of ourselves*
in this hideous city's jungle

        because
        she's cheating on me
        always
        everywhere

and not with
ten
or a hundred
but
with everybody
all at once
and not just
one of her parts
cheats on me
but all of them
each one by itself
with somebody else
so that
even the Jew god
can't be
everywhere at once
the way she is
in her falsehood
everywhere at once
and if you ask me how
I can stand it
I who
love her to distraction
my answer is
every feeling
feeds on itself
jealousy
gradually goes numb
and perhaps burns out
at last
like this insane
love
if Lesbia you'd only sinned
against me enough to make me
suspicious of both good and evil
and through your infamy killed

faithfulness in me for good   and now I'm
almost
like you too
just for that you deserve
terrible endless
agony

[LITTLE TABLETS FOR LESBIA]

YOU DIDN'T COME
WHAT HAPPENED

IF YOU STILL LOVE ME
JUST ONE TINY BIT
LET'S MEET

I HEAR
RANK BILLY-GOAT RUFUS
BANGS YOU

YESTERDAY
TILL DAWN
TOMORROW
TILL DAWN
EXPECTING YOU
FOREVER

[TWO MESSAGES TO IPSITHILLA]

1: my spear's piercing my
   tunic I want you so badly
   fly

2: Lesbia embraced
   me sweet thing
   stay home

[C'S TOAST AT FABULLUS' BANQUET]

hypocrites

you drape the
vulva
like a kneading pan
and never mention
the pastry dough
rising beneath the cloth

though
all of you
always
think about its taste

no matter how chastely-wrapped
the *mater familias'* gown may be
it doesn't in the least deter
the spicy fancies of the guests

even at funerals
they'd rather strip the young widow
with their eyes
than mourn for
the deceased

the vestal's cockeyed devotion
camouflages the *ditch*
that thicket between her thighs
conceals

only my Lesbia
carries hers

[17]

like something she's not ashamed of
covering it just enough
to placate
public prudery

sooner or later
she'll hang
my pendant on it too
like an *ordo*
I hope

[LITTLE TABLETS FOR LESBIA]

MY CUNNING EVENING STAR
WHEN WILL YOU COME BY

THEY SAY
YOU'RE HOT
EVERYONE SATISFIES YOU
BUT ME

RUTHLESS GODDESS
I ADORE YOU

YOU FILTHY WHORE

STICK
WITH YOUR PIMP
OTHO THE BOLD
I SHIT ON YOU BOTH

THERE AREN'T AS MANY POSTS
IN ALL OF GERMANIA'S FORESTS
AS ARE RAMMED INTO YOU
DAILY

ALAS MY LOVE

LESBIA MISERA
MISER CATULLUS

[LESBIA'S LETTER]

I should dismiss your crude epigrams[*] without a word
    because they're as stupid as they are offensive
nevertheless I'll consider my reply[**] a game of distichs
    its meters may dissolve my anger
I've had it with your complaints such whining hurts me
    that wounded male's keening female quaver
confess you're swapping excess for excess
    accusing me again of infidelity
believe you me there's never been a better begetter of infidelity
    than you when Lesbia loved someone else
you managed to seduce a wedded woman from her man
    and buy her heart with your inflammatory songs
where's the breaker of vows where's the unfaithful woman in them
    a glittering halo crowns her sin
when she deceives another with you naturally she's a lady divine
    whereas deceiving you she's instantly a *bestia*
yes she would be too if one iota of the charge you've vilely woven
    against my reputation happened to be true
let me tell you I've had the opportunity more than once
    (I am neither old nor ugly nor poor)

---

[*] She must have been thinking of the following:

> You know no one anymore, you said, but Catullus,
>   preferring me, Lesbia, even over Jupiter.
> I loved you then not just as lovers love the belovèd.
>   but as a father loves his son and son-in-law.
> Now I know you: though you've grown much crueller,
>   and I roast on hotter flames, you mean still less to me.
> You ask, How can that be? My answer is, While such abuse
>   may kindle love, it kills all kindness too.

[**] The reply in verse is probably composed by the poet Egnatius, one of Lesbia's lovers. It is thought to have been a "Catullan game" written by Catullus himself, who wished to experience—in Lesbia's skin—the *other* half of the truth (that was so incomprehensible to him). Yet what follows contradicts that supposition.

to test myself against temptation
  to see if heart and mind would resist
and yet of all who wished to steal from Lesbia
  that forbidden kiss there was never anyone but you
no one in fact succeeded
  as you did undeserved***
        ****
. . . .

*** Perhaps the "most wicked" of all is this epigram:

> Look at Lesbia, my Lesbia, my friend,
> that Lesbia whom Catullus loved
> more than his own, more than himself,
> there at the crossroads, here in the alleys,
> milking the heroic sons of Remus.

**** The rest of the parchment is missing—torn off in a *manner* that suggests violent emotion.

[22]

[C'S LETTER TO A.]

when you come calling
my dear little Aufilena
make sure no one spots you
for god's sake please don't
show up carried
in a sedan chair
the way you'd like
you'll be the talk
of the street
(just as if you came
for your date in a taxi)
people on private business
should stay off the avenue
you don't bang a bass drum
when you're laying an ambush
get here on foot sneak through
the back yard and slip in
by way of the kitchen door
my servants will be given
the day off only my loyal valet
in his little room
to guard our loving
so as we agreed
I expect you Saturday evening
my clever little girl be careful
dear heart think of everything
and if you send a go-between
instruct him
not to shoot off his mouth
because we know
Lesbia's sharp ears
not to mention all those supernumerary ears

(so telephone
with care)

although it's the biggest bonfire
ever heaped up for love
and fidelity has never ever been greater than
what binds me to Lesbia
you ought to be aware that
precisely because this passion surpasses
everything
a hurricane
lashing overhead boiling out of us
it's therefore no surprise if its burning wind
touches so many women
and my Lesbia's also loved
by as many men as she has lovers they say

our faithlessness extends as far
as the vast power of our faithfulness

Possible Impossible Games

how I've lived ever since
Lesbia married me redeemed me
from myself from that tortured and
torturing Catullus that hopeless
clown tripping over a thousand-and-one
fake excuses   now listen to this
dear Calvus let me tell you what life's like now
I'm up early instead of
lolling around cultivating
morbid fantasies in my still half-
dreamy bed I jump out of the warm
covers dash the chill water in
the basin over myself rinse away
last night's remaining crud and head
for the kitchen at a trot where
the cook's laid out
two settings   I grab the tray
load it with milk butter honeycake
whatever Lesbia likes
for breakfast and balancing
skilfully through the rooms I tote
that oddly-amusing burden to my spouse's
bed   feathery kisses by the thousands over her bare
throat over the mound of her breasts over her rounding
plump little belly over her mons shadowed by downy fleece
and upon those little shells I sprinkle throbbing
hot pearls till my darling's halfshut eyes
are sealed
her arms open and fold
around my neck   after breakfast
Lesbia bathes and sits a good half-hour
at her vanity

[25]

trying different hairdos but
finally just pins it up
and slips into a dressing gown
all bright and silly colors purring
like a schoolgirl as she gaily ascends the stairs
her steamy thighs opening and closing
flashing in the spring breeze
we'll leave her there on the terrace   sometimes
she doesn't stir till noon
humming her tunes embroidering reading
not for me though   I'm hard at work
since I've become a married man
and started working I lug so much paper
home you can't even see me behind it
provided I'm home all morning
and don't have to attend a trial
we always lunch together though now and then
Lesbia visits
her dressmaker hairstylist beautician
or drops in on this or that girlfriend
just for some gossip
(which means I have to wait for her)
we take a little siesta
then if there's time for an hour or two
with Lesbia's kids
from her first marriage   because
they can get their lessons
from the Greek slave except for
that extra something without which
all that information's pretty useless
late afternoon or early evening
hours often bring guests
or else we go out
to see some of our acquaintances
me dragging my feet because my heart
senses scarcely a true friend in the whole lot

but Lesbia's mad for them all
and even though aimless folk can't be furnished aims
it gives me a reason to suffer with a smile
midnight's usually past before we're back
home again from those inebriates
though we both water our wine
and sip it slowly
(because we're drunk on each other)
more loving after midnight, you ask, and mornings too?
your day began with lovemaking!
so it did indeed *amice*
and we end it the same way because
the Lesbia–Catullus is so young
young even as this pair of marrieds
I couldn't ask heaven for anything more
than a thousand times a thousand mornings
and a thousand times a thousand nights
for our never-ending thirst and kisses
to be eternal
as long as grass grows green again and again
as long as the tides of the sea flood over and over again

for ten years Lesbia you've been my wife
that dreadful, frenzied jealousy of mine was
calmed long ago it ebbed away forever
we live quietly in a villa
in the rocky landscape of Sabinum
you scold your servants
I put in my day farming
no other cares have we
we're slowly grinding time to bits
through long, long afternoons
and endless, wordless evenings
lounging on the terrace watching
the drowsy herd wend its homeward way
in a cloud of dust

and when the first star of evening flickers
in the sky the servant
lights the lamp down here and we
prepare an early dinner
the darkening hill lulls the smoke
the darkening leaves lull the thrush in its nest
crickets chirp in the garden grass
the hens nod off
our watchdog's dozing too
while we sit and blink at the fire
eyelids heavier and heavier
stray images and troubled dreams
haunt our eyes and hearts
we dream that there was a Rome
and a Lesbia and a Catullus
who did all sorts of crazy things
in the mortal game they played
with a flaming rapier and a poisoned kiss
fighting a fiery duel
once upon a time long long ago

we rouse with a start   bank the fire
tuck ourselves in   till tomorrow

you write Lesbia hoping for news now and then
but Catullus now lives minus news
stars away from your drumming town's
thousand-and-one intrigues and horror stories
well listen girl of our loved/hated Rome
to the way we spend our soft trickling days
with little Ipsithilla
the bride I carried off from Urbs
(who's sauntering into her XX's now)
for your information this is one wild scene though
sometimes rather lovely and even fertile in spots
an old friend and colleague

[28]

returning from these parts recently told me about
a nice little spread on the Aegean shore
for sale cheap
(my inheritance just about covered it)
can you visualize your quondam town lover
out in the fields at daybreak
sweating arguing hectoring the gods
of the lazy old foreman and drowsy hands
anyone knows oxen and buffaloes will pull
but horses can't haul our plows stumbling
over rocks always the fellow dragging
after them soon gives up too
he has to be driven ahead like an animal
and since my heart's the same old one
I get fed up with my landowning
drover's role and prefer to start in
plowing this wretched terrain myself
and the sun's well up in the sky
when, lo! two ponies a little cart
with a lady standing in the cart appear before me
Ipsithilla carrying tasty tidbits in a little hamper
for my breakfast
and the laboring goes on with renewed strength
for a time till noon's upon us
and man and beast are scourged into the shade
by the sun's fiery suffocating force
giddyap my fine fourlegged friend let's rip the wind
from the barren air's caved-in lap
let's gallop home my little Ipsithilla's waiting for us
it's her yes it's her waving to me blushing*

. . . .

. . . .

it's suicide just thinking about it

---

* The rest of the parchment is missing—torn off in a *manner* that suggests violent emotion.

[29]

my self-destructive way of life
all those murderous passions
lodged in my heart all those unbearable
intentions all that fated doom

yet even more ghastly Lesbia is
realizing I'd arranged it all myself because
that was the only means by which you could be
made the executioner of suicidal Catullus
now one by one the lamps go out in me
and in your frenzied existence
that made me think you so
important and yet the most terrible thing for me
is to watch my self-lacerating fantasy fade away
with the multitude of your sins your whoredom
your pleasures that torment Catullus no longer—
what a drab shade you've become

Dependency Games

why should it vex you one and only imperator
if now and then I flash your majestic name
by way of self-exculpation in my poems
on low themes most of them confessions
of this that or the other crush I trust
you don't suppose your name's thrown
down between two Lesbia-ditties like some
challenge or that the same miserable
passion has steamed me up against your power
as against the power of that torturing whore
and above all I hope you don't imagine
I would scribble songs to Lesbia
if just once I could say properly
what I think of you O my emperor

silent tactful midnight
I swear in a whisper to your ear
I'll fulfill what so often I
solemnly swore in vain to do
never again to live enslaved
to the charity of a tyrannical whore
my entire existence dependent
on the flutter of an eyelash
whether I'm to be trashed or
set by some merciful whim at the right hand
no Caesar you shall not be my caesar
no Lesbia Catullus will never
have his despot again
from here on in no despots
I sharpen my knife grind my blade
opposed to your putrefying power
I incite internal dissidence

I swear it whispering to your ear
silent tactful midnight

never Ravidus has a sacred oath
been more heinously broken than your
day-in-day-out disgracing of your vow
so sanctimoniously murmured
into the ears of the gods once upon a time
though any number of no-goods reside
upon the City's seven tumuli all sorts of
burglars brigands thieves
no one both cures and kills at once
even in that scurvy rout there's no such
mongrel scoundrel except for you
I always thought some demon was
having his fun with you (perhaps
because he knew you'd triumph
over him one day casting spells on your
clientele) which is why your
schnozzle's crook'd as queer as
a hunchback's body your body
as queer-shaped as your schnozzola
I divine how your inward distortion's been
manifested in your limbs you maestro
of delusion you feral concocter of venoms
the gods you so meanly defrauded
by swearing to them
(when you took the healer's oath
neither to deceive nor kill)
I wish the gods would show mercy
save this sick betrayed Rome from
you from all her other swindling
physicians

proclaim it by word of mouth scratch it on the walls
"he is not to be counted among Rome's such-and-so-

many (the numbers change constantly) greatest
poets" it could be true for all I know
if anyone but you
Furius spread it about even so
what sane person credits it
because your bias is as blatant
as the fact that you lack talent though
you certainly know how to position yourself
surely you've overheard a thing or two
concerning the history of poetics
and gleaned somewhat from various exemplars
believe me my little Furius a contemporary
confidently picks the good ones from
a plethora of poets only with difficulty
not to mention the greats and from the greats the
greatest ones of all   and this triple sifting's
infallible demanding function
the judging what excels
you presume to be the proud possessor of
forget it Furius don't make me laugh

tomorrow my Catullus you're on
live at 17:50 show up at
Stadium II about five o'clock if you can
because even if there's no harm in
improvising let's have a chat beforehand about a couple
of things for instance whether it's advisable just now
to be calling Egnatius the poetaster by that name
with your old fury
he's Mentula's buddy you know and
through him he's landed a key seat on the
commission for gladiatorial affairs
not to mention the crowd's prime
favorite Mamurra the faggot
your poems dumped a load
of shit on

and of course there's first of all great
Caesar himself glorious benefactor of
the Mamurras and the Mentulas
and whom you had the gall to attack
(for which he'll certainly put
the arena under surveillance)
and if you consider that we all live
by the marketplace showing defiance
to the one who can cut our bread off
is pure madness
to wit handle claque usher patron
never mind what type gently
for your (my, our) own sake
beyond that naturally feel free
to do as you like
nothing and no one stops you
so boldly say whatever's on your mind
when they throw you to the ravenous beasts
tomorrow my Catullus commencing
at 17:50

Unchangeable Changing Games

you say my Calvus no one
had to invent corruption it flourished
in honorable Etruria too
maybe so but tell me where
are the Etruscans now and where now all those
other still more ancient peoples'
children who traded their morals
for silver and gold   extinct
think about it when you ponder
the fate of Rome and not just strutting
bloody destiny   the coral reef
that scuttles our ship
is built up out of unnumbered silly little sins
look at that swinish tax-gatherer
feathering his nest his wife's also a pricked-out creature
if you couldn't tell her from her plum tree
you'd simply think she'd been transplanted here with husband
straight from the hothouse of some plutocrat
but their mingy empty hearts
give them right away they're deadwood-collectors
and not (as they make out) Torch-carrying Pyre-kindlers

they'd have their teeth yanked and
replaced with pearl dentures diamond tiaras
in their hair silver for the gray
and gold for Madame's privy bush
an opaline cenotaph ought to be stood alongside
the sirocco-blasted ruins of her body's nether parts and
purple and velvet ought to fringe that antique
slit so brittle is it the better to be pleasured
they'd like to wreath hubby's heir-raising rod
with a braid of rubies and stick it in a jewel box

these shrewd folks possess a past complete
with phony progenitors paid for with extorted shekels
their purloined ancestral tree goes all the way back to Romulus
not one flunkey to be seen on its branches

they overreach themselves for status they pose they cheat
but you're not fooled if your wits are about

Silo you've got one boring routine
always bad-mouthing the young with your
withered chops because they're not
old and don't live like geronts
"Oh these rotten kids nowadays"
you keep mumbling the way old fogies
complained about you often enough when you were green
by way of compliment
don't you think that's always been the case?
it's just as hard being young
as it is to be old (for different reasons)
hence these two ages seldom understand each other
in point of fact the agèd aren't exempted
from the sins of youth because
here on earth evil is congenital
descending from father to son   lest it be forgot

you're the shame of Rome Gellius you
catamite you wretched thing still young in
years but taking your putridity into account
quite a bit older than plenty of cynical old roués
and so overripe good for nothing but spitting on
perhaps there's not one sin your dæmon
could warn you against and if all of them put together
don't weigh down your soul it's because
you're harboring in that poor tenement of flesh
a spirit equally false frightened
and pusillanimous

[36]

truer and more loyal souls than yours have died
disgusting deaths by strict command punished
for their sins few of the foulest felons
could outdo you in perverse passion
your uncombed locks and the barrette binding
that dirty cascade of hair over your shoulders
and all the baubles (fake gold and glass gems)
chains bracelets earrings garish
shawls all those little hanging buckles and straps
and your whole get-up as though it's a cover
on principle (or should I call it a philosophy)
yet just scratch your "principle"
and pus oozes out the lazy filth
and if some samaritans suppose
you're a golden boy they're wrong
like gold you may be yellow but still a rancid pulp

just a generation perhaps two and even fame
decays   o the shame   to our fathers' heroic beautiful
example   they were ready
to give their lives in a dignified cause
but alas is there any cause now worth
sacrificing life for and if so is there
anyone who'd ever die
defying death faithful to a sacred cause
even if the republic itself were at stake
great deeds shall not come to pass here
indifferently we endure the wars
forced upon us and with an apathetic heart
a man dies for himself his cloak
pulled over his face   no hero merely a victim
what bound us together is going
to pieces   we only think of Number One

Resurrection Games

while copying Catullus
[GLOSSED BY A 14TH CENTURY FRIAR]

knowe that this hapless felawe served his master Satanas thorowe lustfulle lecherie and therebye mordered his owne soule by cause of his sinne and so wonne himself to helle. *five Pater Nostres and also sevene Ave Marias moghte be told for him.*

By another, and later, hand

do you with loue rede it, for it is most louelie

Laudatio Mulierum

that is

*Of Womman hire preyse**

ayenst that auncyen
barbèd-voysed Catullus
whose herte was by a womman
made most biter

euer since the worlde was worlde
and man knew wommankinde
fools and sages bothe have hurlid
their curs ayenst oure god

the yonge in all their pryde
the olde in spyteful glee
sound men ther eyen open wide
and hunchbacks deceivèd so murilie

for why? they al declare that she,
the flour of earthes first dayes
grew fillèd full with lecherie
whenas sinne came thorowe hire wayes

since what time a fiendish vessel
boyles up in wommans lap with frothe
its smoke daubs al with soot
a thicke and heavy shame its brothe

---

* Translation of a Latin poem by a late medieval Hungarian cleric.

[41]

ensamples endlesse ther weel may be
and yet I say ther stille is oon
and oon onlie cas I swer
falsèd with lying accusacioun

and that euerich man names
his owne sin and also it confesses
when he laies on the tendre partener
the weyt of his owne wekenesses

what we finde is lakkede greuous
are saye we hire wrongs and fautes
on hire we hang whats missed by us
lyk a paupers filthy clouts

thogh hire lap be more swete
than goddes ambrosial breeth
in hire cavitie is lyf concealèd
as also is the kiss of deeth

plesure grief the font
of eueri thing that was and is
or shal ever be—their sorse lies
in those swete and gracious curves

whateuer *ab urbe condita*
may in chronicles lie gravèd
it cannot be *historia*
whateuer actes whateuer dedes

what philosophies and credes
the thousand andswers to *id est*
al preoes for al theorikes
are to nothing crushed by *yis*

and lykewise with the deuels *no*
that grete schadwes negatif
lyf is necessarie also
that it may be negatived

and so must she be preysed
the procreatif part of creacion
the wardein of this holi flame
and verrai sorse of oure poor race

and tribute to hire lap be paied
whether virgin or a hore-queans
for lyf is what she wishes
bifore al other or any thing

mans work sholde be to plow hire
and to sow hire yeer by yeer
and wommans work lyk that of erthes
must neuer ask wherfore

In Which Lesbia to Julia's Liken'd

This illnesse, these damnable doings Venus
    decrees but to punish mee
bring with them no balme; my heart, meseemes,
    such sentence cannot dree,
th' which I must paye out, and beare my life
    and soule so bitterlie.

Should some enquire, What's ruin'd the garden
    of my heart? I've this reply:
A wick'd master that thinkes to torture mee
    with dagger, with evil, and for why?
To promote damnation as my portion, since
    Hell's the place for such as I.

My pain is hard, my early death,
    th'antique poet suffer'd,
liv'd thorow, wrote, and in his owne way
    his owne doom discover'd
before Lord Christ: from all time's ocean streame,
    his example to mee's offer'd.

Catullus his bitter sonets of Lesbia sang
    in the clerkes' learnèd tongue,
whilst I in Magyar the Cruell Faire beseeche,
    and for her favours long;
Lesbia and Julia, Julia and Lesbia, which is
    which? It's one same song.

Then take them bothe, these females
    compos'd of fire and ice:
adore them, clasp them in thine armes, or else
    let thy poignard suffice;

[45]

of him who's true they make an outlaw grim, or, oh,
      a fugitive head with a price!

In times to come, and in far off lands,
      their names will eccho'd bee,
as long as Love treads out the heart,
      so long shall live their memorie,
because their lives do make men err,
      and lose eternall mercie.

And you that sorrow, who warre within, or
      waste in rosie pleasure,
shall not feare in Time to look upon our fate,
      rememb'ring our desir'd treasure:
then thinke how our love, our searing passion remains,
      and will remaine, forever.

A Griefe for Mihály Vitéz

A lonelie heart in sorrow wails
over the grave of Mihály Vitéz[*]
    in mourning for him whose
bodie now lies devour'd by death
in this deep hole, in the black earth
    of Hajduság.

Gratefulnesse brings mee to visit where
your bodie moulders to mud here,
    to kneel by your crumbling hand;
teacher, brother, and mentor too,
such are you called by a friend who's true,
    a poet too, Vitéz.

You see, Mihály, now that you can see
—says this friend—what we cannot see,
    more especially, what can be seen:
that shee became your fatall destinie,
more than yourself you lov'd that shee—
    Catullus's Lesbia.

---

[*] Mihály Vitéz Csokonai (1773–1805), poet and dramatist, lived about as long as did Catullus. His poetry displays the characteristics of classicism, together with elements of folk poetry. His praise of solitude and nature worship echo Rousseau, whom he admired. In 1797 he met Julianna Vajda, who is the 'Lilla' of his poems, but was prevented by her father from marrying her. Never in good health, his poverty and limited success in publication depressed him. He caught cold giving a funeral sermon in Nagyvárad, Transylvania, and died of pneumonia. The best lyric poet of the Hungarian Literary Revival, his writing displayed a versatility and artistry in versification new in Hungarian poetry. He was the first true researcher and specialist in Hungarian forms and meters.

    It might be remarked here that I have put Rákos' poems eulogizing Csokonai into forms resembling those in Donne's *Songs & Sonets* because the language used in the Hungarian is asynchronously parallel to the Early Modern English of about 1610. Similarly, Rákos' simulation of the language of the mediaeval Hungarian cleric of the fifteenth century is parallel to the Middle English of Chaucer's youth, that is, the language of about 1350. (Translators's note.)

You suffer'd so and sans salvation
on the crosse of ignoble emotion,
        and all the world
laugh'd at your agonie; as she did often too,
shee, for whom your wounded form they threw
        down into the dust.

Lilla, Lilla, Vitéz was mayhap your lov'd one,
you let him hope, mayhap, and led him on;
        still, 'twas on your account
he found nowhere in his adopt'd land
nor house, nor home, no place to stand,
        and all because of you.

I mourne you, my poët, I grieve for you,
because you gave yourself over to sorrow,
        and thence to earth;
by wine persecuted, and by love, you,
our holie, outcaste Mihály—we know
        what losing you has cost!

Had but capricious Fortune been inclin'd:
thou jewel, thou treasure of Arpád's land,
        thou rare, Hungarian non pareill—
but you were captive to such ill-luck,
and madlie roam'd about, like a strayed dogge
        kick'd from pillar to post.

And yet to thee I call loudlie:
thou need'st not wait for some twenty-third centurie
        to be known for what thou art!
ev'n now thy radiant genius the heav'ns
illumines with thy poems,
        where thy etheriall image glows!

Yet onlie your body decaies down there,
oh Poët-God, for your creating pow'r

immortall is and eternall!
You fashion'd a world, and like the soule
of the Lord you float, as did He of old,
farre, farre above its waters.

The Resurrection of the Poet Catullus

When the ruined body of poor Catullus[*]
had moldered away into dust,
a sad, mad efflorescence revelled
and rioted in orgy over his grave.

When the hand that inscribed
immortal love on tablets
was rotting in an urn,
the song of the thrush rang out in joy.

When barbarian boots trampled
both Rome and tablets down, a flame
flared where purple kisses took refuge
as it had once in his songs.

When the City lay locked dead still
and glowing eyes alone could plead
the suppressed rights of desire,
the setting sun awakened him.

And when on that night of nights
a young man spat the name, Lesbia!
in his whore's face, poor Catullus
was resurrected then forever.

---

[*] On the back of the text of the verses The Death of the Poet Catullus.

Dissecting Kisses

Naked? Yet beneath your dress
your flesh lies too.
I'd like to strip you
to your bare bones.

And suppose your bones lie, too?
Their nakedness is not enough.
I'd crush your bones open, gaze
into their throbbing marrow.

That would bring final knowledge!
Though not even then. Because the
most ferocious, dissecting kiss
cannot expose all of your lies.

Naked? You wear flesh like your dress!
You hide it—and it conceals, it lies.
Just once I'd like to take you down
to your bare bones.

Because knowing's not enough, no matter
what excitement your cunt offers.
While you hold me, I want to see
your very marrow under the microscope.

To see your innermost secrets projected
plate by plate on the X-ray screen
as we kiss, showing all
the wreckage of your lies.

Epilogue I

so many Catulluses—day after day
always one day older today
I'm yesterday's older brother just as
he's older than that one of the day before and so on
back from my first toga to my toddling
time   so many so many Catulluses
you my lovely younger brother as you were
you my lovely younger brother as I was
before that line of all the Catulluses
fading in fog (a file of pines
on the Appian Way) looking at those thirty odd years
of myself I wonder if out of that thousand
and ten thousand Catulluses
there's one to spit on
what a phony world I lived in I really don't
think there's anything for me to be ashamed of
you dwindle away nobly in the living fire
of your hearts o my younger brothers the sun
shoots its rays at you and day by day
with the sun you die the death by fire
I just wish your older brothers my future
selves' Catulluses could perish
with the same blazing heart

Epilogue II

let's just say that by experimentation
by exquisite fine-tuning
he picked up a trace of something
antedating his period by centuries
but couldn't prove it
there are discoveries in love too
and a great many believers die at the stake
before one or two cosmic obscenities
get laid down in law books

Epilogue III

      a black flutter of wings
your moment above time's shoreless
torrent and now its shadow trembles forever
on the watery mirror 'when we sometimes
feel a bittersweet weight on the chest
we know you felt it too
and gave it a name naming
many other things till then also nameless and
dumb and a torment to man because
he could not speak to it
though it was what he wanted above all nameless
and wordless he had merely *lived* his inner
stories obscurely until you flared up
a cluster of lights in utter darkness that rend us
even now some of your trail-blazing words
still glow no way to lose them
odi et amo appalling
I hate and I love if we
didn't know it was human too like
that curse *a lioness gave you birth*
or the sobriquet *defututa* whorehouse-begot
and thrown like a necklace of nettles
over a girl's head and your suppressed
choking cry over a brother's grave
frater ave atque vale and so you seal up
the solitary life of the dead and the living
you flit over pasts and times to come
alive you flit by the bluffs
of the centuries in your nightblack cloak poet

Sándor Rákos was born in 1921, in Ujfehértó-Kálmánháza, northeastern Hungary, son of a village schoolteacher. He studied economics in Budapest, but took no degree; worked in various administrative, journalistic and editorial jobs; has devoted himself to writing since 1952. He heads the Translators' Section of the Hungarian Writers' Union.

Meztelen arc (Naked Face), a first collection of poems, appeared in 1971. There followed *Az emlék jelene* (Memory's Present), 1973; *Elforgó eg* (The Sky Turns Away), essays, 1974; *Harc a madárral* (Fighting the Bird), poems, 1980; *Társasmonológ* (Soliloquy with Others), poems, 1982; *A tüz kérlelése* (Imploring Fire), collected poems, 1984. Has translated *Gilgamesh* and other pieces of Mesopotamian poetry, and a volume of folk poems from the South Sea Islands.